I0384694

JUST LIKE A CHILD WHO WAS FORMED IN THE WOMB, THIS PRAYER JOURNAL IN YOUR HANDS WAS BIRTHED FROM MY SOUL!
MAY YOU RECEIVE THE SAME JOY I HAD CREATING IT! - FaB -

PERSONAL PRAYER JOURNAL
WWW.FABTHEAUTHOR.COM
FIRST PUBLISHED IN 2022

TEXT AND ILLUSTRATIONS COPYRIGHT FUZEKIDZ UNLIMITED INC., 2022 ALL RIGHTS RESERVED. NO PART OF THIS PUBLICATION MAY BE REPRODUCED OR TRANSMITTED IN ANY FORM OR BY ANY MEANS, ELECTRONIC OR MECHANICAL, INCLUDING PHOTOGRAPHY, RECORDING, STORAGE IN AN INFORMATION RETRIEVAL SYSTEM, OR OTHERWISE, WITHOUT THE PRIOR WRITTEN PERMISSION OF THE PUBLISHER, EXCEPT IN THE CASE OF BRIEF QUOTATION EMBODIED IN CRITICAL REVIEWS AND CERTAIN OTHER NON-COMMERCIAL USES PERMITTED BY THE UNITED STATES OF AMERICA COPYRIGHT LAW.

TO CONTACT THE AUTHOR, PLEASE EMAIL AUTHORFABLOVE@GMAIL.COM.
ISBN 978-1-7355691-5-4

"LET THE MORNING BRING ME WORD OF YOUR UNFAILING LOVE, FOR I HAVE PUT MY TRUST IN YOU. SHOW ME THE WAY I SHOULD GO, FOR TO YOU I ENTRUST MY LIFE."
~PSALMS 143:8 (NIV)

DEAR ME,
I PROMISE TO DEVOTE MYSELF WHOLEHEARTEDLY TO GETTING CLOSER TO GOD FOR THE NEXT 30 (31) DAYS.

SIGNATURE

DATE

" TRUST IN THE LORD WITH ALL YOUR HEART AND LEAN NOT ON YOUR OWN UNDERSTANDING."
~PROVERBS 3:5 (NIV)

"THE ANGEL WENT TO HER AND SAID, "GREETINGS, YOU WHO ARE HIGHLY FAVORED! THE LORD IS WITH YOU.""
~LUKE 1:28 (NIV)

WHEN YOU PRAY
MATTHEW 6:9-13 (NIV)

PRAISE GOD FOR WHO HE IS AND WHAT HE HAS DONE.

"OUR FATHER IN HEAVEN, HALLOWED BE YOUR NAME."

REPENT OF SINS I HAVE COMMITTED.

"AND FORGIVE US OUR DEBTS, AS WE ALSO HAVE FORGIVEN OUR DEBTORS."

ASK FOR THE NEEDS OF OTHERS AND FOR MY NEEDS.

"GIVE US TODAY OUR DAILY BREAD. AND LEAD US NOT INTO TEMPTATION, BUT DELIVER US FROM THE EVIL ONE."

YIELD MY WILL TO GOD'S WILL. CHANGE MY PLANS TO GOD'S PLANS FOR ME.

"YOUR KINGDOM COME, YOUR WILL BE DONE, ON EARTH AS IT IS IN HEAVEN."

MAY I PRAY FOR YOU?

HEAVENLY FATHER,

I UPLIFT YOUR SON OR DAUGHTER READING THIS PRAYER. I ASK THAT YOU LEAD THEM IN THE WAY THAT THEY SHOULD GO. HELP THEM TO HEAR, SEE, AND WRITE WHAT YOU WISH FOR THEM TO KNOW TO GROW AND DO YOUR WILL. I PRAY THAT THEY GIVE YOU THE PRAISE, HONOR, AND GLORY AS YOU SHOW UP BIG IN THEIR LIFE AS THEY BEGIN THEIR NEW JOURNEY TO STUDY AND GET CLOSER TO YOU!

IN JESUS NAME,
AMEN

IF YOU RATHER WRITE A PRAYER FOR YOURSELF AND BLESSING FOR YOUR STUDIES, DO SO BELOW.

_____
_____
_____
_____
_____
_____
_____
_____
_____

I'M BELIEVING GOD FOR:
WEEK 1

_____
_____
_____
_____
_____
_____
_____
_____
_____
_____
_____
_____
_____
_____
_____
_____
_____
_____
_____
_____

"BLESSED IS SHE WHO HAS BELIEVED THAT THE LORD WOULD FULFILL HIS PROMISES TO HER!"
~LUKE 1:45 (NIV)

Daily Devotional

"SHOW ME YOUR WAYS, LORD, TEACH ME YOUR PATHS. (5) GUIDE ME IN YOUR TRUTH AND TEACH ME, FOR YOU ARE GOD MY SAVIOR, AND MY HOPE IS IN YOU ALL DAY LONG..." ~PSALMS 25:4-5 (NIV)

DATE: _____

VERSE OF THE DAY

REFLECTION OF THE DAY

PRAYER OF THE DAY

"THE LORD IS NOT SLOW IN KEEPING HIS PROMISE, AS SOME UNDERSTAND SLOWNESS. INSTEAD HE IS PATIENT WITH YOU, NOT WANTING ANYONE TO PERISH, BUT EVERYONE TO COME TO REPENTANCE." ~2 PETER 3:9 (NIV)

"THE LORD IS NOT SLOW IN KEEPING HIS PROMISE, AS SOME UNDERSTAND SLOWNESS. INSTEAD HE IS PATIENT WITH YOU, NOT WANTING ANYONE TO PERISH, BUT EVERYONE TO COME TO REPENTANCE."~2 PETER 3:9 (NIV)

"YOUR WORD IS A LAMP TO GUIDE MY FEET AND A LIGHT FOR MY PATH."
~PSALM 119:105 (NIV)

Daily Devotional

"SHOW ME YOUR WAYS, LORD, TEACH ME YOUR PATHS. (5) GUIDE ME IN YOUR TRUTH AND TEACH ME, FOR YOU ARE GOD MY SAVIOR, AND MY HOPE IS IN YOU ALL DAY LONG..." ~PSALMS 25:4-5 (NIV)

DATE: _____

VERSE OF THE DAY

REFLECTION OF THE DAY

PRAYER OF THE DAY

"THE LORD IS NOT SLOW IN KEEPING HIS PROMISE, AS SOME UNDERSTAND SLOWNESS. INSTEAD HE IS PATIENT WITH YOU, NOT WANTING ANYONE TO PERISH, BUT EVERYONE TO COME TO REPENTANCE." ~2 PETER 3:9 (NIV)

"THE LORD IS NOT SLOW IN KEEPING HIS PROMISE, AS SOME UNDERSTAND SLOWNESS. INSTEAD HE IS PATIENT WITH YOU, NOT WANTING ANYONE TO PERISH, BUT EVERYONE TO COME TO REPENTANCE." ~2 PETER 3:9 (NIV)

WE ARE "CREATED IN CHRIST JESUS UNTO GOOD WORKS, WHICH GOD HATH BEFORE ORDAINED THAT WE SHOULD WALK IN THEM."
~EPHESIANS 2:10 (NIV)

Daily Devotional

"SHOW ME YOUR WAYS, LORD, TEACH ME YOUR PATHS. (5) GUIDE ME IN YOUR TRUTH AND TEACH ME, FOR YOU ARE GOD MY SAVIOR, AND MY HOPE IS IN YOU ALL DAY LONG..." ~PSALMS 25:4-5 (NIV)

DATE: _____

VERSE OF THE DAY

REFLECTION OF THE DAY

PRAYER OF THE DAY

"THE LORD IS NOT SLOW IN KEEPING HIS PROMISE, AS SOME UNDERSTAND SLOWNESS. INSTEAD HE IS PATIENT WITH YOU, NOT WANTING ANYONE TO PERISH, BUT EVERYONE TO COME TO REPENTANCE." ~2 PETER 3:9 (NIV)

"THE LORD IS NOT SLOW IN KEEPING HIS PROMISE, AS SOME UNDERSTAND SLOWNESS. INSTEAD HE IS PATIENT WITH YOU, NOT WANTING ANYONE TO PERISH, BUT EVERYONE TO COME TO REPENTANCE." ~2 PETER 3:9 (NIV)

"BUT YOU WILL RECEIVE POWER WHEN THE HOLY SPIRIT COMES ON YOU..."
~ACTS 1:8 (NIV)

Daily Devotional

"SHOW ME YOUR WAYS, LORD, TEACH ME YOUR PATHS. (5) GUIDE ME IN YOUR TRUTH AND TEACH ME, FOR YOU ARE GOD MY SAVIOR, AND MY HOPE IS IN YOU ALL DAY LONG..." ~PSALMS 25:4-5 (NIV)

DATE: _____

VERSE OF THE DAY

REFLECTION OF THE DAY

PRAYER OF THE DAY

"THE LORD IS NOT SLOW IN KEEPING HIS PROMISE, AS SOME UNDERSTAND SLOWNESS. INSTEAD HE IS PATIENT WITH YOU, NOT WANTING ANYONE TO PERISH, BUT EVERYONE TO COME TO REPENTANCE." ~2 PETER 3:9 (NIV)

"THE LORD IS NOT SLOW IN KEEPING HIS PROMISE, AS SOME UNDERSTAND SLOWNESS. INSTEAD HE IS PATIENT WITH YOU, NOT WANTING ANYONE TO PERISH, BUT EVERYONE TO COME TO REPENTANCE." ~2 PETER 3:9 (NIV)

"THE THIEF COMES ONLY TO STEAL AND KILL AND DESTROY; I HAVE COME THAT THEY MAY HAVE LIFE, AND HAVE IT TO THE FULL."
~JOHN 10:10 (NIV)

Daily Devotional

"SHOW ME YOUR WAYS, LORD, TEACH ME YOUR PATHS. (5) GUIDE ME IN YOUR TRUTH AND TEACH ME, FOR YOU ARE GOD MY SAVIOR, AND MY HOPE IS IN YOU ALL DAY LONG..." ~PSALMS 25:4-5 (NIV)

DATE: _____

VERSE OF THE DAY

REFLECTION OF THE DAY

PRAYER OF THE DAY

"THE LORD IS NOT SLOW IN KEEPING HIS PROMISE, AS SOME UNDERSTAND SLOWNESS. INSTEAD HE IS PATIENT WITH YOU, NOT WANTING ANYONE TO PERISH, BUT EVERYONE TO COME TO REPENTANCE."~2 PETER 3:9 (NIV)

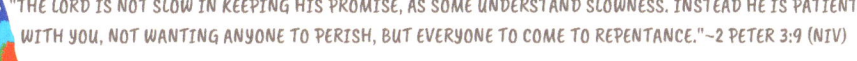

"THE LORD IS NOT SLOW IN KEEPING HIS PROMISE, AS SOME UNDERSTAND SLOWNESS. INSTEAD HE IS PATIENT WITH YOU, NOT WANTING ANYONE TO PERISH, BUT EVERYONE TO COME TO REPENTANCE." ~2 PETER 3:9 (NIV)

"BUT THE LORD IS FAITHFUL, AND HE WILL STRENGTHEN YOU AND PROTECT YOU FROM THE EVIL ONE."
~2 THESSALONIANS 3:3 (NIV)

Daily Devotional

"SHOW ME YOUR WAYS, LORD, TEACH ME YOUR PATHS. (5) GUIDE ME IN YOUR TRUTH AND TEACH ME, FOR YOU ARE GOD MY SAVIOR, AND MY HOPE IS IN YOU ALL DAY LONG..." ~PSALMS 25:4-5 (NIV)

DATE: _____

VERSE OF THE DAY

REFLECTION OF THE DAY

PRAYER OF THE DAY

"THE LORD IS NOT SLOW IN KEEPING HIS PROMISE, AS SOME UNDERSTAND SLOWNESS. INSTEAD HE IS PATIENT WITH YOU, NOT WANTING ANYONE TO PERISH, BUT EVERYONE TO COME TO REPENTANCE." ~2 PETER 3:9 (NIV)

"THE LORD IS NOT SLOW IN KEEPING HIS PROMISE, AS SOME UNDERSTAND SLOWNESS. INSTEAD HE IS PATIENT WITH YOU, NOT WANTING ANYONE TO PERISH, BUT EVERYONE TO COME TO REPENTANCE." ~2 PETER 3:9 (NIV)

"BEING CONFIDENT OF THIS, THAT HE WHO BEGAN A GOOD WORK IN YOU WILL CARRY IT ON TO COMPLETION UNTIL THE DAY OF CHRIST JESUS."
~PHILIPPIANS 1:6 (NIV)

Daily Devotional

"SHOW ME YOUR WAYS, LORD, TEACH ME YOUR PATHS. (5) GUIDE ME IN YOUR TRUTH AND TEACH ME, FOR YOU ARE GOD MY SAVIOR, AND MY HOPE IS IN YOU ALL DAY LONG..." ~PSALMS 25:4-5 (NIV)

DATE: _____

VERSE OF THE DAY

REFLECTION OF THE DAY

PRAYER OF THE DAY

"THE LORD IS NOT SLOW IN KEEPING HIS PROMISE, AS SOME UNDERSTAND SLOWNESS. INSTEAD HE IS PATIENT WITH YOU, NOT WANTING ANYONE TO PERISH, BUT EVERYONE TO COME TO REPENTANCE." ~2 PETER 3:9 (NIV)

"THE LORD IS NOT SLOW IN KEEPING HIS PROMISE, AS SOME UNDERSTAND SLOWNESS. INSTEAD HE IS PATIENT WITH YOU, NOT WANTING ANYONE TO PERISH, BUT EVERYONE TO COME TO REPENTANCE." ~2 PETER 3:9 (NIV)

"I WILL GIVE YOU A NEW HEART AND PUT A NEW SPIRIT IN YOU; I WILL REMOVE FROM YOU YOUR HEART OF STONE AND GIVE YOU A HEART OF FLESH."~EZEKIEL 36:26 (NIV)

PRAISE REPORT(S)

"BUT THOSE WHO HOPE IN THE LORD WILL RENEW THEIR STRENGTH. THEY WILL SOAR ON WINGS LIKE EAGLES; THEY WILL RUN AND NOT GROW WEARY, THEY WILL WALK AND NOT BE FAINT."
ISAIAH 40:31 NIV

I'M BELIEVING GOD FOR:
WEEK 2

_____
_____
_____
_____
_____
_____
_____
_____
_____
_____
_____
_____
_____
_____
_____
_____
_____
_____

"BLESSED IS SHE WHO HAS BELIEVED THAT THE LORD WOULD FULFILL HIS PROMISES TO HER!"
~LUKE 1:45 (NIV)

"MAY THE GOD OF HOPE
FILL YOU WITH ALL JOY
AND PEACE AS YOU TRUST
IN HIM, SO THAT YOU
MAY OVERFLOW WITH
HOPE BY THE POWER OF
THE HOLY SPIRIT."
~ROMANS 15:13 (NIV)

Daily Devotional

"SHOW ME YOUR WAYS, LORD, TEACH ME YOUR PATHS. (5) GUIDE ME IN YOUR TRUTH AND TEACH ME, FOR YOU ARE GOD MY SAVIOR, AND MY HOPE IS IN YOU ALL DAY LONG..." ~PSALMS 25:4-5 (NIV)

DATE: _____

VERSE OF THE DAY

REFLECTION OF THE DAY

PRAYER OF THE DAY

"THE LORD IS NOT SLOW IN KEEPING HIS PROMISE, AS SOME UNDERSTAND SLOWNESS. INSTEAD HE IS PATIENT WITH YOU, NOT WANTING ANYONE TO PERISH, BUT EVERYONE TO COME TO REPENTANCE." ~2 PETER 3:9 (NIV)

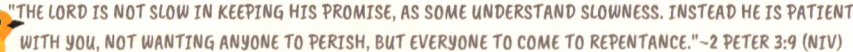

"THE LORD IS NOT SLOW IN KEEPING HIS PROMISE, AS SOME UNDERSTAND SLOWNESS. INSTEAD HE IS PATIENT WITH YOU, NOT WANTING ANYONE TO PERISH, BUT EVERYONE TO COME TO REPENTANCE." ~2 PETER 3:9 (NIV)

"THE TONGUE HAS THE POWER OF LIFE AND DEATH, AND THOSE WHO LOVE IT WILL EAT ITS FRUIT."
~PROVERBS 18:21 (NIV)

Daily Devotional

"SHOW ME YOUR WAYS, LORD, TEACH ME YOUR PATHS. (5) GUIDE ME IN YOUR TRUTH AND TEACH ME, FOR YOU ARE GOD MY SAVIOR, AND MY HOPE IS IN YOU ALL DAY LONG..." ~PSALMS 25:4-5 (NIV)

DATE: _____

VERSE OF THE DAY

REFLECTION OF THE DAY

PRAYER OF THE DAY

"THE LORD IS NOT SLOW IN KEEPING HIS PROMISE, AS SOME UNDERSTAND SLOWNESS. INSTEAD HE IS PATIENT WITH YOU, NOT WANTING ANYONE TO PERISH, BUT EVERYONE TO COME TO REPENTANCE." ~2 PETER 3:9 (NIV)

"THE LORD IS NOT SLOW IN KEEPING HIS PROMISE, AS SOME UNDERSTAND SLOWNESS. INSTEAD HE IS PATIENT WITH YOU, NOT WANTING ANYONE TO PERISH, BUT EVERYONE TO COME TO REPENTANCE." ~2 PETER 3:9 (NIV)

"BUT THE FRUIT OF THE SPIRIT IS LOVE, JOY, PEACE, FORBEARANCE, KINDNESS, GOODNESS, FAITHFULNESS, GENTLENESS AND SELF-CONTROL. AGAINST SUCH THINGS THERE IS NO LAW."~GALATIANS 5:22-23 (NIV)

Daily Devotional

"SHOW ME YOUR WAYS, LORD, TEACH ME YOUR PATHS. (5) GUIDE ME IN YOUR TRUTH AND TEACH ME, FOR YOU ARE GOD MY SAVIOR, AND MY HOPE IS IN YOU ALL DAY LONG..." ~PSALMS 25:4-5 (NIV)

DATE: _____

VERSE OF THE DAY

REFLECTION OF THE DAY

PRAYER OF THE DAY

"THE LORD IS NOT SLOW IN KEEPING HIS PROMISE, AS SOME UNDERSTAND SLOWNESS. INSTEAD HE IS PATIENT WITH YOU, NOT WANTING ANYONE TO PERISH, BUT EVERYONE TO COME TO REPENTANCE." ~2 PETER 3:9 (NIV)

"THE LORD IS NOT SLOW IN KEEPING HIS PROMISE, AS SOME UNDERSTAND SLOWNESS. INSTEAD HE IS PATIENT WITH YOU, NOT WANTING ANYONE TO PERISH, BUT EVERYONE TO COME TO REPENTANCE." ~2 PETER 3:9 (NIV)

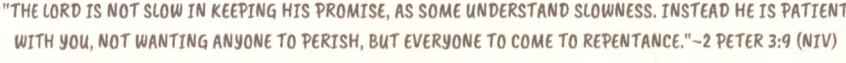

"I CAN DO ALL THINGS THROUGH CHRIST WHICH STRENGTHENETH ME."
~PHILIPPIANS 4:13 (KJV)

Daily Devotional

"SHOW ME YOUR WAYS, LORD, TEACH ME YOUR PATHS. (5) GUIDE ME IN YOUR TRUTH AND TEACH ME, FOR YOU ARE GOD MY SAVIOR, AND MY HOPE IS IN YOU ALL DAY LONG..." ~PSALMS 25:4-5 (NIV)

DATE: _____

VERSE OF THE DAY

REFLECTION OF THE DAY

PRAYER OF THE DAY

"THE LORD IS NOT SLOW IN KEEPING HIS PROMISE, AS SOME UNDERSTAND SLOWNESS. INSTEAD HE IS PATIENT WITH YOU, NOT WANTING ANYONE TO PERISH, BUT EVERYONE TO COME TO REPENTANCE." ~2 PETER 3:9 (NIV)

"THE LORD IS NOT SLOW IN KEEPING HIS PROMISE, AS SOME UNDERSTAND SLOWNESS. INSTEAD HE IS PATIENT WITH YOU, NOT WANTING ANYONE TO PERISH, BUT EVERYONE TO COME TO REPENTANCE." ~2 PETER 3:9 (NIV)

"CAST ALL YOUR ANXIETY ON HIM BECAUSE HE CARES FOR YOU."
~1 PETER 5:7 (NIV)

Daily Devotional

"SHOW ME YOUR WAYS, LORD, TEACH ME YOUR PATHS. (5) GUIDE ME IN YOUR TRUTH AND TEACH ME, FOR YOU ARE GOD MY SAVIOR, AND MY HOPE IS IN YOU ALL DAY LONG..." ~PSALMS 25:4-5 (NIV)

DATE: _____

VERSE OF THE DAY

REFLECTION OF THE DAY

PRAYER OF THE DAY

"THE LORD IS NOT SLOW IN KEEPING HIS PROMISE, AS SOME UNDERSTAND SLOWNESS. INSTEAD HE IS PATIENT WITH YOU, NOT WANTING ANYONE TO PERISH, BUT EVERYONE TO COME TO REPENTANCE." ~2 PETER 3:9 (NIV)

"THE LORD IS NOT SLOW IN KEEPING HIS PROMISE, AS SOME UNDERSTAND SLOWNESS. INSTEAD HE IS PATIENT WITH YOU, NOT WANTING ANYONE TO PERISH, BUT EVERYONE TO COME TO REPENTANCE." ~2 PETER 3:9 (NIV)

"GOD IS OUR REFUGE AND STRENGTH, AN EVER-PRESENT HELP IN TROUBLE."
~PSALMS 46:1 (NIV)

Daily Devotional

"SHOW ME YOUR WAYS, LORD, TEACH ME YOUR PATHS. (5) GUIDE ME IN YOUR TRUTH AND TEACH ME, FOR YOU ARE GOD MY SAVIOR, AND MY HOPE IS IN YOU ALL DAY LONG..."~PSALMS 25:4-5 (NIV)

DATE: _____

VERSE OF THE DAY

REFLECTION OF THE DAY

PRAYER OF THE DAY

"THE LORD IS NOT SLOW IN KEEPING HIS PROMISE, AS SOME UNDERSTAND SLOWNESS. INSTEAD HE IS PATIENT WITH YOU, NOT WANTING ANYONE TO PERISH, BUT EVERYONE TO COME TO REPENTANCE." ~2 PETER 3:9 (NIV)

"THE LORD IS NOT SLOW IN KEEPING HIS PROMISE, AS SOME UNDERSTAND SLOWNESS. INSTEAD HE IS PATIENT WITH YOU, NOT WANTING ANYONE TO PERISH, BUT EVERYONE TO COME TO REPENTANCE." ~2 PETER 3:9 (NIV)

"FOR I KNOW THE PLANS I HAVE FOR YOU," DECLARES THE LORD, "PLANS TO PROSPER YOU AND NOT TO HARM YOU, PLANS TO GIVE YOU HOPE AND A FUTURE."
~JEREMIAH 29:11 (NIV)

Daily Devotional

"SHOW ME YOUR WAYS, LORD, TEACH ME YOUR PATHS. (5) GUIDE ME IN YOUR TRUTH AND TEACH ME, FOR YOU ARE GOD MY SAVIOR, AND MY HOPE IS IN YOU ALL DAY LONG..." ~PSALMS 25:4-5 (NIV)

DATE: _____

VERSE OF THE DAY

REFLECTION OF THE DAY

PRAYER OF THE DAY

"THE LORD IS NOT SLOW IN KEEPING HIS PROMISE, AS SOME UNDERSTAND SLOWNESS. INSTEAD HE IS PATIENT WITH YOU, NOT WANTING ANYONE TO PERISH, BUT EVERYONE TO COME TO REPENTANCE." ~2 PETER 3:9 (NIV)

"THE LORD IS NOT SLOW IN KEEPING HIS PROMISE, AS SOME UNDERSTAND SLOWNESS. INSTEAD HE IS PATIENT WITH YOU, NOT WANTING ANYONE TO PERISH, BUT EVERYONE TO COME TO REPENTANCE." ~2 PETER 3:9 (NIV)

"THEREFORE DO NOT WORRY ABOUT TOMORROW, FOR TOMORROW WILL WORRY ABOUT ITSELF. EACH DAY HAS ENOUGH TROUBLE OF ITS OWN."
~MATTHEW 6:34 (NIV)

PRAISE REPORT(S)

"BUT THOSE WHO HOPE IN THE LORD WILL RENEW THEIR STRENGTH. THEY WILL SOAR ON WINGS LIKE EAGLES; THEY WILL RUN AND NOT GROW WEARY, THEY WILL WALK AND NOT BE FAINT."
ISAIAH 40:31 NIV

I'M BELIEVING GOD FOR:
WEEK 3

"BLESSED IS SHE WHO HAS BELIEVED THAT THE LORD WOULD FULFILL HIS PROMISES TO HER!"
~LUKE 1:45 (NIV)

"COMMIT TO THE LORD WHATEVER YOU DO, AND HE WILL ESTABLISH YOUR PLANS."
~PROVERBS 16:3 (NIV)

Daily Devotional

"SHOW ME YOUR WAYS, LORD, TEACH ME YOUR PATHS. (5) GUIDE ME IN YOUR TRUTH AND TEACH ME, FOR YOU ARE GOD MY SAVIOR, AND MY HOPE IS IN YOU ALL DAY LONG..." ~PSALMS 25:4-5 (NIV)

DATE: _____

VERSE OF THE DAY

REFLECTION OF THE DAY

PRAYER OF THE DAY

"THE LORD IS NOT SLOW IN KEEPING HIS PROMISE, AS SOME UNDERSTAND SLOWNESS. INSTEAD HE IS PATIENT WITH YOU, NOT WANTING ANYONE TO PERISH, BUT EVERYONE TO COME TO REPENTANCE." ~2 PETER 3:9 (NIV)

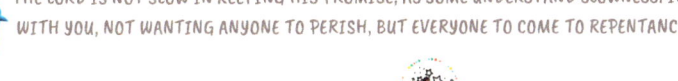
"THE LORD IS NOT SLOW IN KEEPING HIS PROMISE, AS SOME UNDERSTAND SLOWNESS. INSTEAD HE IS PATIENT WITH YOU, NOT WANTING ANYONE TO PERISH, BUT EVERYONE TO COME TO REPENTANCE." ~2 PETER 3:9 (NIV)

"GIVE THANKS TO THE LORD, FOR HE IS GOOD; HIS LOVE ENDURES FOREVER."
~1 CHRONICLES 16:34 (NIV)

Daily Devotional

"SHOW ME YOUR WAYS, LORD, TEACH ME YOUR PATHS. (5) GUIDE ME IN YOUR TRUTH AND TEACH ME, FOR YOU ARE GOD MY SAVIOR, AND MY HOPE IS IN YOU ALL DAY LONG..." ~PSALMS 25:4-5 (NIV)

DATE: _____

VERSE OF THE DAY

REFLECTION OF THE DAY

PRAYER OF THE DAY

 "THE LORD IS NOT SLOW IN KEEPING HIS PROMISE, AS SOME UNDERSTAND SLOWNESS. INSTEAD HE IS PATIENT WITH YOU, NOT WANTING ANYONE TO PERISH, BUT EVERYONE TO COME TO REPENTANCE." ~2 PETER 3:9 (NIV)

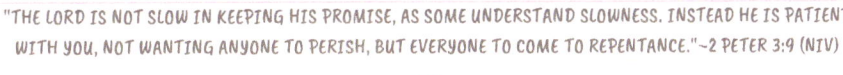
"THE LORD IS NOT SLOW IN KEEPING HIS PROMISE, AS SOME UNDERSTAND SLOWNESS. INSTEAD HE IS PATIENT WITH YOU, NOT WANTING ANYONE TO PERISH, BUT EVERYONE TO COME TO REPENTANCE."~2 PETER 3:9 (NIV)

"SO DO NOT FEAR, FOR I AM WITH YOU; DO NOT BE DISMAYED, FOR I AM YOUR GOD. I WILL STRENGTHEN YOU AND HELP YOU; I WILL UPHOLD YOU WITH MY RIGHTEOUS RIGHT HAND."
~ISAIAH 41:10 (NIV)

Daily Devotional

"SHOW ME YOUR WAYS, LORD, TEACH ME YOUR PATHS. (5) GUIDE ME IN YOUR TRUTH AND TEACH ME, FOR YOU ARE GOD MY SAVIOR, AND MY HOPE IS IN YOU ALL DAY LONG..." ~PSALMS 25:4-5 (NIV)

DATE: _____

VERSE OF THE DAY

REFLECTION OF THE DAY

PRAYER OF THE DAY

"THE LORD IS NOT SLOW IN KEEPING HIS PROMISE, AS SOME UNDERSTAND SLOWNESS. INSTEAD HE IS PATIENT WITH YOU, NOT WANTING ANYONE TO PERISH, BUT EVERYONE TO COME TO REPENTANCE."~2 PETER 3:9 (NIV)

"THE LORD IS NOT SLOW IN KEEPING HIS PROMISE, AS SOME UNDERSTAND SLOWNESS. INSTEAD HE IS PATIENT WITH YOU, NOT WANTING ANYONE TO PERISH, BUT EVERYONE TO COME TO REPENTANCE." ~2 PETER 3:9 (NIV)

"DO NOT BE ANXIOUS ABOUT ANYTHING, BUT IN EVERY SITUATION, BY PRAYER AND PETITION, WITH THANKSGIVING, PRESENT YOUR REQUESTS TO GOD. (7) AND THE PEACE OF GOD, WHICH TRANSCENDS ALL UNDERSTANDING, WILL GUARD YOUR HEARTS AND YOUR MINDS IN CHRIST JESUS.."
~PHILIPPIANS 4:6–7 (NIV)

Daily Devotional

"SHOW ME YOUR WAYS, LORD, TEACH ME YOUR PATHS. (5) GUIDE ME IN YOUR TRUTH AND TEACH ME, FOR YOU ARE GOD MY SAVIOR, AND MY HOPE IS IN YOU ALL DAY LONG..." ~PSALMS 25:4-5 (NIV)

DATE: _____

VERSE OF THE DAY

REFLECTION OF THE DAY

PRAYER OF THE DAY

"THE LORD IS NOT SLOW IN KEEPING HIS PROMISE, AS SOME UNDERSTAND SLOWNESS. INSTEAD HE IS PATIENT WITH YOU, NOT WANTING ANYONE TO PERISH, BUT EVERYONE TO COME TO REPENTANCE." ~2 PETER 3:9 (NIV)

"THE LORD IS NOT SLOW IN KEEPING HIS PROMISE, AS SOME UNDERSTAND SLOWNESS. INSTEAD HE IS PATIENT WITH YOU, NOT WANTING ANYONE TO PERISH, BUT EVERYONE TO COME TO REPENTANCE." ~2 PETER 3:9 (NIV)

"AND NOW THESE THREE REMAIN: FAITH, HOPE AND LOVE. BUT THE GREATEST OF THESE IS LOVE."
~1 CORINTHIANS 13:13 (NIV)

Daily Devotional

"SHOW ME YOUR WAYS, LORD, TEACH ME YOUR PATHS. (5) GUIDE ME IN YOUR TRUTH AND TEACH ME, FOR YOU ARE GOD MY SAVIOR, AND MY HOPE IS IN YOU ALL DAY LONG..." ~PSALMS 25:4-5 (NIV)

DATE: _____

VERSE OF THE DAY

REFLECTION OF THE DAY

PRAYER OF THE DAY

"THE LORD IS NOT SLOW IN KEEPING HIS PROMISE, AS SOME UNDERSTAND SLOWNESS. INSTEAD HE IS PATIENT WITH YOU, NOT WANTING ANYONE TO PERISH, BUT EVERYONE TO COME TO REPENTANCE." ~2 PETER 3:9 (NIV)

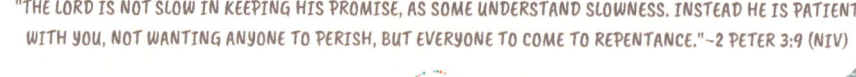

"THE LORD IS NOT SLOW IN KEEPING HIS PROMISE, AS SOME UNDERSTAND SLOWNESS. INSTEAD HE IS PATIENT WITH YOU, NOT WANTING ANYONE TO PERISH, BUT EVERYONE TO COME TO REPENTANCE." ~2 PETER 3:9 (NIV)

"CONSEQUENTLY, FAITH COMES FROM HEARING THE MESSAGE, AND THE MESSAGE IS HEARD THROUGH THE WORD ABOUT CHRIST."
~ROMANS 10:17 (NIV)

Daily Devotional

"SHOW ME YOUR WAYS, LORD, TEACH ME YOUR PATHS. (5) GUIDE ME IN YOUR TRUTH AND TEACH ME, FOR YOU ARE GOD MY SAVIOR, AND MY HOPE IS IN YOU ALL DAY LONG..." ~PSALMS 25:4-5 (NIV)

DATE: _____

VERSE OF THE DAY

REFLECTION OF THE DAY

PRAYER OF THE DAY

"THE LORD IS NOT SLOW IN KEEPING HIS PROMISE, AS SOME UNDERSTAND SLOWNESS. INSTEAD HE IS PATIENT WITH YOU, NOT WANTING ANYONE TO PERISH, BUT EVERYONE TO COME TO REPENTANCE." ~2 PETER 3:9 (NIV)

 "THE LORD IS NOT SLOW IN KEEPING HIS PROMISE, AS SOME UNDERSTAND SLOWNESS. INSTEAD HE IS PATIENT WITH YOU, NOT WANTING ANYONE TO PERISH, BUT EVERYONE TO COME TO REPENTANCE." ~2 PETER 3:9 (NIV)

"FOR GOD SO LOVED THE WORLD THAT HE GAVE HIS ONE AND ONLY SON, THAT WHOEVER BELIEVES IN HIM SHALL NOT PERISH BUT HAVE ETERNAL LIFE."
~JOHN 3:16 (NIV)

Daily Devotional

"SHOW ME YOUR WAYS, LORD, TEACH ME YOUR PATHS. (5) GUIDE ME IN YOUR TRUTH AND TEACH ME, FOR YOU ARE GOD MY SAVIOR, AND MY HOPE IS IN YOU ALL DAY LONG..." ~PSALMS 25:4-5 (NIV)

DATE: _____

VERSE OF THE DAY

REFLECTION OF THE DAY

PRAYER OF THE DAY

"THE LORD IS NOT SLOW IN KEEPING HIS PROMISE, AS SOME UNDERSTAND SLOWNESS. INSTEAD HE IS PATIENT WITH YOU, NOT WANTING ANYONE TO PERISH, BUT EVERYONE TO COME TO REPENTANCE."~2 PETER 3:9 (NIV)

"THE LORD IS NOT SLOW IN KEEPING HIS PROMISE, AS SOME UNDERSTAND SLOWNESS. INSTEAD HE IS PATIENT WITH YOU, NOT WANTING ANYONE TO PERISH, BUT EVERYONE TO COME TO REPENTANCE." ~2 PETER 3:9 (NIV)

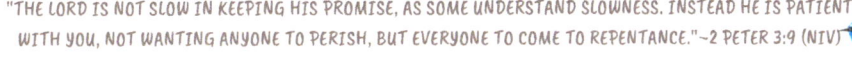

"FOR GOD HATH NOT GIVEN US THE SPIRIT OF FEAR; BUT OF POWER, AND OF LOVE, AND OF A SOUND MIND."
~2 TIMOTHY 1 (KJV)

PRAISE REPORT(S)

"BUT THOSE WHO HOPE IN THE LORD WILL RENEW THEIR STRENGTH. THEY WILL SOAR ON WINGS LIKE EAGLES; THEY WILL RUN AND NOT GROW WEARY, THEY WILL WALK AND NOT BE FAINT."
ISAIAH 40:31 NIV

I'M BELIEVING GOD FOR:
WEEK 4

"BLESSED IS SHE WHO HAS BELIEVED THAT THE LORD WOULD FULFILL HIS PROMISES TO HER!"
~LUKE 1:45 (NIV)

"I PRAISE YOU BECAUSE I AM FEARFULLY AND WONDERFULLY MADE; YOUR WORKS ARE WONDERFUL, I KNOW THAT FULL WELL."
~PSALM 139:14 (NIV)

Daily Devotional

"SHOW ME YOUR WAYS, LORD, TEACH ME YOUR PATHS. (5) GUIDE ME IN YOUR TRUTH AND TEACH ME, FOR YOU ARE GOD MY SAVIOR, AND MY HOPE IS IN YOU ALL DAY LONG..." ~PSALMS 25:4-5 (NIV)

DATE: _____

VERSE OF THE DAY

REFLECTION OF THE DAY

PRAYER OF THE DAY

"THE LORD IS NOT SLOW IN KEEPING HIS PROMISE, AS SOME UNDERSTAND SLOWNESS. INSTEAD HE IS PATIENT WITH YOU, NOT WANTING ANYONE TO PERISH, BUT EVERYONE TO COME TO REPENTANCE." ~2 PETER 3:9 (NIV)

"THE LORD IS NOT SLOW IN KEEPING HIS PROMISE, AS SOME UNDERSTAND SLOWNESS. INSTEAD HE IS PATIENT WITH YOU, NOT WANTING ANYONE TO PERISH, BUT EVERYONE TO COME TO REPENTANCE." ~2 PETER 3:9 (NIV)

"SUBMIT YOURSELVES, THEN, TO GOD. RESIST THE DEVIL, AND HE WILL FLEE FROM YOU."
~JAMES 4:7 (NIV)

Daily Devotional

"SHOW ME YOUR WAYS, LORD, TEACH ME YOUR PATHS. (5) GUIDE ME IN YOUR TRUTH AND TEACH ME, FOR YOU ARE GOD MY SAVIOR, AND MY HOPE IS IN YOU ALL DAY LONG..." ~PSALMS 25:4-5 (NIV)

DATE: _____

VERSE OF THE DAY

REFLECTION OF THE DAY

PRAYER OF THE DAY

"THE LORD IS NOT SLOW IN KEEPING HIS PROMISE, AS SOME UNDERSTAND SLOWNESS. INSTEAD HE IS PATIENT WITH YOU, NOT WANTING ANYONE TO PERISH, BUT EVERYONE TO COME TO REPENTANCE." ~2 PETER 3:9 (NIV)

"THE LORD IS NOT SLOW IN KEEPING HIS PROMISE, AS SOME UNDERSTAND SLOWNESS. INSTEAD HE IS PATIENT WITH YOU, NOT WANTING ANYONE TO PERISH, BUT EVERYONE TO COME TO REPENTANCE." ~2 PETER 3:9 (NIV)

"NO WEAPON FORGED AGAINST YOU WILL PREVAIL, AND YOU WILL REFUTE EVERY TONGUE THAT ACCUSES YOU..." ~ISAIAH 54:17 (NIV)

Daily Devotional

"SHOW ME YOUR WAYS, LORD, TEACH ME YOUR PATHS. (5) GUIDE ME IN YOUR TRUTH AND TEACH ME, FOR YOU ARE GOD MY SAVIOR, AND MY HOPE IS IN YOU ALL DAY LONG..." ~PSALMS 25:4-5 (NIV)

DATE: _____

VERSE OF THE DAY

REFLECTION OF THE DAY

PRAYER OF THE DAY

 "THE LORD IS NOT SLOW IN KEEPING HIS PROMISE, AS SOME UNDERSTAND SLOWNESS. INSTEAD HE IS PATIENT WITH YOU, NOT WANTING ANYONE TO PERISH, BUT EVERYONE TO COME TO REPENTANCE." ~2 PETER 3:9 (NIV)

"THE LORD IS NOT SLOW IN KEEPING HIS PROMISE, AS SOME UNDERSTAND SLOWNESS. INSTEAD HE IS PATIENT WITH YOU, NOT WANTING ANYONE TO PERISH, BUT EVERYONE TO COME TO REPENTANCE." ~2 PETER 3:9 (NIV)

"DO NOT BE OVERCOME BY EVIL, BUT OVERCOME EVIL WITH GOOD."
~ROMANS 12:21 (NIV)

Daily Devotional

"SHOW ME YOUR WAYS, LORD, TEACH ME YOUR PATHS. (5) GUIDE ME IN YOUR TRUTH AND TEACH ME, FOR YOU ARE GOD MY SAVIOR, AND MY HOPE IS IN YOU ALL DAY LONG..." ~PSALMS 25:4-5 (NIV)

DATE: _____

VERSE OF THE DAY

REFLECTION OF THE DAY

PRAYER OF THE DAY

"THE LORD IS NOT SLOW IN KEEPING HIS PROMISE, AS SOME UNDERSTAND SLOWNESS. INSTEAD HE IS PATIENT WITH YOU, NOT WANTING ANYONE TO PERISH, BUT EVERYONE TO COME TO REPENTANCE." ~2 PETER 3:9 (NIV)

"THE LORD IS NOT SLOW IN KEEPING HIS PROMISE, AS SOME UNDERSTAND SLOWNESS. INSTEAD HE IS PATIENT WITH YOU, NOT WANTING ANYONE TO PERISH, BUT EVERYONE TO COME TO REPENTANCE." ~2 PETER 3:9 (NIV)

"FOR GOD SO LOVED THE WORLD THAT HE GAVE HIS ONE AND ONLY SON, THAT WHOEVER BELIEVES IN HIM SHALL NOT PERISH BUT HAVE ETERNAL LIFE."
~JOHN 3:16 (NIV)

Daily Devotional

"SHOW ME YOUR WAYS, LORD, TEACH ME YOUR PATHS. (5) GUIDE ME IN YOUR TRUTH AND TEACH ME, FOR YOU ARE GOD MY SAVIOR, AND MY HOPE IS IN YOU ALL DAY LONG..." ~PSALMS 25:4-5 (NIV)

DATE: _____

VERSE OF THE DAY

REFLECTION OF THE DAY

PRAYER OF THE DAY

"THE LORD IS NOT SLOW IN KEEPING HIS PROMISE, AS SOME UNDERSTAND SLOWNESS. INSTEAD HE IS PATIENT WITH YOU, NOT WANTING ANYONE TO PERISH, BUT EVERYONE TO COME TO REPENTANCE." ~2 PETER 3:9 (NIV)
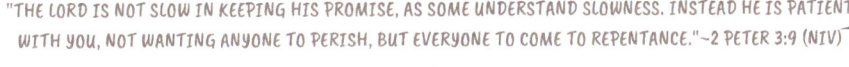

"THE LORD IS NOT SLOW IN KEEPING HIS PROMISE, AS SOME UNDERSTAND SLOWNESS. INSTEAD HE IS PATIENT WITH YOU, NOT WANTING ANYONE TO PERISH, BUT EVERYONE TO COME TO REPENTANCE." ~2 PETER 3:9 (NIV)

"IN THEIR HEARTS HUMANS PLAN THEIR COURSE, BUT THE LORD ESTABLISHES THEIR STEPS."
~PROVERBS 16:9 (NIV)

Daily Devotional

"SHOW ME YOUR WAYS, LORD, TEACH ME YOUR PATHS. (5) GUIDE ME IN YOUR TRUTH AND TEACH ME, FOR YOU ARE GOD MY SAVIOR, AND MY HOPE IS IN YOU ALL DAY LONG..." ~PSALMS 25:4-5 (NIV)

DATE: _____

VERSE OF THE DAY

REFLECTION OF THE DAY

PRAYER OF THE DAY

"THE LORD IS NOT SLOW IN KEEPING HIS PROMISE, AS SOME UNDERSTAND SLOWNESS. INSTEAD HE IS PATIENT WITH YOU, NOT WANTING ANYONE TO PERISH, BUT EVERYONE TO COME TO REPENTANCE." ~2 PETER 3:9 (NIV)

"THE LORD IS NOT SLOW IN KEEPING HIS PROMISE, AS SOME UNDERSTAND SLOWNESS. INSTEAD HE IS PATIENT WITH YOU, NOT WANTING ANYONE TO PERISH, BUT EVERYONE TO COME TO REPENTANCE." ~2 PETER 3:9 (NIV)

"BLESSED ARE YOU WHO HUNGER NOW, FOR YOU WILL BE SATISFIED. BLESSED ARE YOU WHO WEEP NOW, FOR YOU WILL LAUGH."
~LUKE 6:21 (NIV)

Daily Devotional

"SHOW ME YOUR WAYS, LORD, TEACH ME YOUR PATHS. (5) GUIDE ME IN YOUR TRUTH AND TEACH ME, FOR YOU ARE GOD MY SAVIOR, AND MY HOPE IS IN YOU ALL DAY LONG..." ~PSALMS 25:4-5 (NIV)

DATE: _____

VERSE OF THE DAY

REFLECTION OF THE DAY

PRAYER OF THE DAY

"THE LORD IS NOT SLOW IN KEEPING HIS PROMISE, AS SOME UNDERSTAND SLOWNESS. INSTEAD HE IS PATIENT WITH YOU, NOT WANTING ANYONE TO PERISH, BUT EVERYONE TO COME TO REPENTANCE." ~2 PETER 3:9 (NIV)

"THE LORD IS NOT SLOW IN KEEPING HIS PROMISE, AS SOME UNDERSTAND SLOWNESS. INSTEAD HE IS PATIENT WITH YOU, NOT WANTING ANYONE TO PERISH, BUT EVERYONE TO COME TO REPENTANCE." ~2 PETER 3:9 (NIV)

"IF WE CONFESS OUR SINS, HE IS FAITHFUL AND JUST AND WILL FORGIVE US OUR SINS AND PURIFY US FROM ALL UNRIGHTEOUSNESS."
~1 JOHN 1:9 (NIV)

Daily Devotional

"SHOW ME YOUR WAYS, LORD, TEACH ME YOUR PATHS. (5) GUIDE ME IN YOUR TRUTH AND TEACH ME, FOR YOU ARE GOD MY SAVIOR, AND MY HOPE IS IN YOU ALL DAY LONG..." ~PSALMS 25:4-5 (NIV)

DATE: _____

VERSE OF THE DAY

REFLECTION OF THE DAY

PRAYER OF THE DAY

"THE LORD IS NOT SLOW IN KEEPING HIS PROMISE, AS SOME UNDERSTAND SLOWNESS. INSTEAD HE IS PATIENT WITH YOU, NOT WANTING ANYONE TO PERISH, BUT EVERYONE TO COME TO REPENTANCE." ~2 PETER 3:9 (NIV)

"THE LORD IS NOT SLOW IN KEEPING HIS PROMISE, AS SOME UNDERSTAND SLOWNESS. INSTEAD HE IS PATIENT WITH YOU, NOT WANTING ANYONE TO PERISH, BUT EVERYONE TO COME TO REPENTANCE."~2 PETER 3:9 (NIV)

JESUS ANSWERED, "I AM THE WAY AND THE TRUTH AND THE LIFE. NO ONE COMES TO THE FATHER EXCEPT THROUGH ME."
~JOHN 14:6 (NIV)

PRAISE REPORT(S)

"BUT THOSE WHO HOPE IN THE LORD WILL RENEW THEIR STRENGTH. THEY WILL SOAR ON WINGS LIKE EAGLES; THEY WILL RUN AND NOT GROW WEARY, THEY WILL WALK AND NOT BE FAINT."
ISAIAH 40:31 NIV

HOW I'VE GROWN SPIRITUALLY:

"WHEN I WAS A CHILD, I TALKED LIKE A CHILD, I THOUGHT LIKE A CHILD, I REASONED LIKE A CHILD. WHEN I BECAME A MAN, I PUT THE WAYS OF CHILDHOOD BEHIND ME."
1 CORINTHIANS 13:11 NIV

"His master replied, 'Well done, good and faithful servant! You have been faithful with a few things; I will put you in charge of many things. Come and share your master's happiness!"
~Matthew 25:23 (NIV)

PRAYER CHALLENGE BINGO

TO EXTEND YOUR SPIRITUAL GROWTH, PRAY FOR A VARIETY OF AREAS WITH THIS BINGO CHALLENGE CARD. YOU CAN DO IT ON YOUR OWN OR WITH A GROUP.

Pray for a sibling	Pray for a co-worker	Pray for a parent	Pray for your boss	Pray for a friend
Pray for healing	Pray for wisdom	Pray for peace	Pray for mental health	Pray for a loving heart
Pray for forgiveness	Pray for purity	Pray for motivation	Pray for awareness of truth	Pray for unshakable faith
Pray for the lost	Pray for your neighbor	Pray for the Lord's will in your life	Pray for patience	Pray for Kingdom vision
Pray for humility	Pray for your job	Pray for fresh spiritual hunger	Pray for direction	Pray for an obedient heart
Pray for ears to hear His voice	Pray for a deeper relationship with God	Pray for generosity	Pray for a grateful heart	Pray for protection

GIVE THANKS

AND PRAISE

Every day is a blessing

www.ingramcontent.com/pod-product-compliance
Lightning Source LLC
Chambersburg PA
CBHW041216070526
44583CB00001B/2